Brewology

Brewology

An Illustrated Dictionary
for Beer Lovers

Cheers from,
Mark Brewer
2017

Mark Brewer

Foreword by Guy Gilchrist, artist and writer of the syndicated comic strip *Nancy*

Skyhorse Publishing

Skyhorse Publishing books may be purchased in bulk at special discounts for sales promotion, corporate gifts, fund-raising, or educational purposes. Special editions can also be created to specifications. For details, contact the Special Sales Department, Skyhorse Publishing, 307 West 36th Street, 11th Floor, New York, NY 10018 or info@ skyhorsepublishing.com.

Skyhorse® and Skyhorse Publishing® are registered trademarks of Skyhorse Publishing, Inc.®, a Delaware corporation.

Visit our website at www.skyhorsepublishing.com.

10 9 8 7 6 5 4 3 2

Library of Congress Cataloging-in-Publication Data is available on file.

Cover design by Mark Brewer

Print ISBN: 978-1-63220-659-6
Ebook ISBN: 978-1-63220-889-7

Printed in China

The only thing I love more than drinking a craft beer, is sharing one with my family and friends. Thank you for your love and support.

—Mark xo

Foreword

A Toast! To Mark Brewer! Creative Genius, Beer Drinker! And not necessarily in that order!

When Mark asked me to write a foreword to *Brewology*, I jumped at the chance. Not because of my well-known love of beer, but because of my admiration and love for the author. I consider Mark to be my second son. I have known Mark since he was about 15.

I remember well the day he came by my Connecticut studio with about 20 pounds of cartoon sketches under his arm, and big dreams in his head. I remember I looked through his artwork and sent him home with about a month's worth of art lessons from me as "homework." I watched him walk out my studio door with the idea I would never see him again. After all, I had given assignments like this to many aspiring artists who wished to work with me, and the vast majority just quit and never did the work and never got back in touch. I was a pretty tough teacher. After all, cartooning is a pretty tough business.

So imagine my surprise when this kid showed up at my door with a month's worth of drawing lessons done in a week! While still going to school full-time! I knew right then that Mark Brewer was special and that he wanted a career in cartooning and humorous illustration. He had *it*. The desire. That feeling inside you that turns dreams into reality. That need down deep that makes wanting to draw and write and entertain people your oxygen.

I took Mark on as a student at my studio, giving him art lessons and a small salary in return for him sweeping and cleaning the studio, running errands, and, if there was time left in the day, possibly helping on backgrounds and erasing one of the many projects we had going—from my Mudpie and Tiny Dinos children's books, to Teenage Mutant Ninja Turtles, to Disney, to Muppet Babies. Within two weeks, Mark was working on the Disney stuff right alongside me and my veteran staff artists!

I never in my life had seen, and still have not seen after all these years, a more driven, hard-working, creative force of nature than Mark Brewer! Mark has endless talent—that is for sure—but when you combine that talent with his drive and "never quit" attitude and a pure love of cartooning, you have the perfect recipe for success!

Mark and I went on to work on many wonderful projects together through those early years of his career, and, yes, we shared a good many beers. We both also play guitar and sing and write country music, so there have been many a beer sung about as well!

I truly have loved reading this new book of Mark's that you hold in one hand, with your brew of choice in a frosty mug in the other! So, while we all hoist a cold one, let me make a toast! To Mark Brewer! Cartoonist, illustrator, country singer, and master of brewology! Long may you rock!

Oh, and Mark? The bar tab is on you this time.

Guy Gilchrist

A BRIEF HISTORY OF BEER
(A true gift from the gods)

Beer is one of the oldest beverages known to man . . . and woman! In fact, women were the first brewers, since one of their primary responsibilities involved cooking. Years ago beer was considered a food as well as a drink. Beer provided many of the calories needed for one's daily diet. Dating back all the way to the fifth millennium BC, beer was recorded by the Ancient Egyptian scribes, who also created an extra hieroglyph specifically for "brewer." Historians tell us that beer was used as a method to compensate laborers who were building the pyramids. And would you believe that if an Egyptian man offered a woman a sip of his brew and she accepted, they were betrothed? Try that move on a woman today, and you're lucky to get out of the situation with only a few bruises. My question is how did these marriages fare in the years to follow, after the women graduated from sips to gulps to eventually handing him back an empty mug?

It has been said that Noah requested beer on his ark, and around 4300 BC the Babylonians recorded nearly twenty different types of beer recipes on clay tablets. Back then, water was not always clean and most certainly not as filtered as it is now. Some of it contained bacteria and parasites, which caused people to get sick. Many even died from drinking water. But you wouldn't die if you drank beer! Since the beer brewing process requires the water to be boiled, beer was a pure drink. It was powerful enough to be used for medicinal purposes, proper enough to be presented as a gift to the Egyptian Pharaohs, and great enough to be sacrificed to the gods. Early civilizations believed the altering effects that beer had on them were supernatural. Intoxication was purely divine, and the drink as a whole was considered a gift from the gods. Many of us still believe this today!

Egyptians produced beer by fermenting bread or grain, and added dates to improve the taste. It was cloudy and completely unfiltered. Because there were no natural preservatives used in the process, beer had a short shelf life. While celebrating together, early cultures often drank beer from a communal bowl using reed straws to avoid ingesting the grain hulls and other sediment in the brew.

With the rise of Christianity and the cultivation of barley came a more mature brewing process. Christian monks played an important role in the production of beer as they used their knowledge of agriculture and science to refine the brewing process. Not only did they brew beer for trading purposes, but monks also provided beer to visiting travelers and offered their breweries for shelter. Consequently, there are a number of Christian saints who are patrons of brewing, including Saint Augustine of Hippo, Saint Luke the Evangelist, and Saint Nicholas, among others.

Prior to brewers using hops to preserve beer, bark or leaves were used. Gruit, which is a combination of herbs and spices, was used sometime after bark and leaves to flavor and preserve beer. Although some forms of gruit still exist today, it was never an equal match for the preservative that hops is. The first recorded use of hops was in 1079 in Germany. By the thirteenth century, hops began to be more commonly used than gruit to flavor and preserve beer. Soon after, hops would become the most widespread ingredient used as a preservative. In 1516, German brewers from Bavaria enacted the Reinheitsgebot purity law, which stated that only water, malted barley, and hops (this was before yeast was understood) were permitted to be used in the brewing process. This law not only assured local beer drinkers and consumers all around the world that German beers were of the highest quality; it also gave Germany a reputation for a brewing craftsmanship that exists to this day. The world-famous Oktoberfest fair, held in Munich each September since 1810, still allows only beer that has been brewed under the Reinheitsgebot standard to be served.

In 1620 the Pilgrims landed in Plymouth Rock carrying beer with them. It's safe to assume beer was served at the first Thanksgiving gathering. Beer was the main beverage back then. Both George Washington and Thomas Jefferson brewed their own beer. We all know that Sam Adams did too, although that's not the founding father's recipe we're drinking. That's Jim Koch's family beer recipe, which is another topic for another day. Hmmm, perhaps another book?

By the 1800s immigrants from Germany were bringing their brewing expertise to their new home, America. In the 1800s, Louis Pasteur discovered the role yeast played in the fermentation process while educating others on how it worked. Although yeast was already being used as an ingredient in brewing and is essential to the process, its importance had not yet been fully realized until then. To this day, the main ingredients in beer have not changed. They consist of water, grain (mostly malted barley), hops, and yeast. With the development of commercial refrigeration, automatic bottling, and pasteurization in the late 1800s came the big brands of beer. Some of these brands are still around today, many of which taste and look the same. There is speculation that the reason these big beer companies' brews all taste and look similar is because they are from recipes dating back to when women were the primary brewers in the kitchen. And since women preferred a lighter beer to a hearty meal in a glass . . . voila! I know what you're thinking—"this is just another example of how women run this world." Well, keep it to yourself, guys!

Around 1880 there were approximately 2,300 breweries in the United States. By 1914 the larger commercial breweries drove the number of smaller operations down to around 1,400. Since then, these brewing conglomerates have worked hard to get us to drink the same commercial lagers over and over again. In fact, the only thing that ever changes is the can or bottle they put their brew in. I think it's really interesting that the scar from 1914 is still prevalent today, even though craft brewing is growing by leaps and bounds. Next time you walk into a store to buy beer, notice all the space that just one of the big brewing companies takes up. Then look at the puny amount of space your favorite craft brewing company gets. Craft brewers provide quality beer brewed with interesting ingredients that produce all sorts of unique tastes to satisfy most any palette. Big beer marketers provide gimmicks of wide-mouthed, frost-brewed liner cans that are cold-mountain-filtered. They also provide fun commercials that show off the latest line of bikinis. Now there's an interesting ingredient!

Perhaps the only thing more devastating to the American beer industry was Prohibition—the nationwide ban on the production of all alcoholic beverages in effect from 1921 to 1933. By 1935 there was said to be only 160 operational breweries left in existence because of this. By the year 1960, fewer than 60 had survived. Flavorful beer was an endangered species that was almost as extinct as the T-Rex!

I have one last bit of factual history to include that I find remarkable. This final bit of history is something that you and I are experiencing right now. Around the early 1990s in the United States, craft breweries started popping up everywhere. Even as I write this in 2014, breweries are multiplying faster than brewer's yeast can turn sugar into alcohol. Despite a few big commercial companies offering cool cans of beer without taste, we have the largest variety of flavorful beer to choose that we have ever had. I like to think that the ghosts and descendants of the brewers who were shut down by the big commercial operations back in the early 1900s are responsible for the throng of breweries popping up today. Back to reclaim what is rightfully theirs. Sweet (or maybe in this case, bitter) revenge that you and I get to enjoy in every glass. Statistics currently show that more than 35 billion gallons of beer are produced globally each year with a revenue greater than 300 billion dollars. Nearly one-third of that revenue is attributed to the American consumer who has asked and continues to receive some of the best beer from the most qualified brewers all over the world. Let's drink to that (like we need an excuse)!

Mark Brewer

Brewology

Abbey Beer \ˈa-bē ˈbir\: A type of beer originally brewed by monks in monasteries, in a method that came to be known as the monastic brewing style. In modern times the term *abbey beer* has come to be known as any beer made or presented in a monastic style but without having to actually be brewed in monasteries or controlled by monks. In 1999 an official label certifying *Belgian Abbey Beers* was established to distinguish the monasteries that still brew or control aspects of the brewing operation from the breweries that only imply religious connections without actually being in a monastery or under any monastic supervision.

Abbey Beer

Additive \ˈa-də-tiv\: An ingredient added to simplify the brewing process, prolong the shelf life, or impart a specific flavor of characteristic of a beer. Beer produced strictly under the Reinheitsgebot (German Beer Purity Law) cannot contain additives. Often beer that is naturally carbonated or bottled with living yeasts in it will not have additives due to the fact that they would kill any living yeast.

Adjunct \ˈa-ˌjəŋ(k)t\: A non-essential ingredient used in beer to supplement the main grain ingredient in the mash. An adjunct can be used to cheapen the cost of production overall as well as to enhance the flavor. In addition to adjuncts being unmalted grains such as corn, oats, barley, and wheat, they may also be spices used for flavoring such as chocolate, nutmeg, orange, coffee, and pumpkin.

Adjunct

Aging \ˈāj ēn\: The amount of time various types of beer are left to mature.
Over months and even years the flavors of a freshly brewed beer start
to change primarily due to oxidation. Hop flavors fade over time while
beers with a high alcohol content (ABV) tend to mature quite nicely. Both
light and heat will speed up oxidation so aging in a dark place with a cool
temperature between 50 and 55°F is optimal.

Alcohol \ˈal-kə-ˌhȯl\: When yeast converts starches into sugar during the
fermentation process it produces this intoxicating byproduct.

Alcohol By Volume (ABV) \ˈal-kə-hȯl ˈbī ˈväl-yüm\: A measurement used
to determine the percentage of alcohol within the beer in terms of volume.
The measurement is sometimes indicated on the product in the abbreviated
form, *ABV*.

Aging

Alcohol By Volume

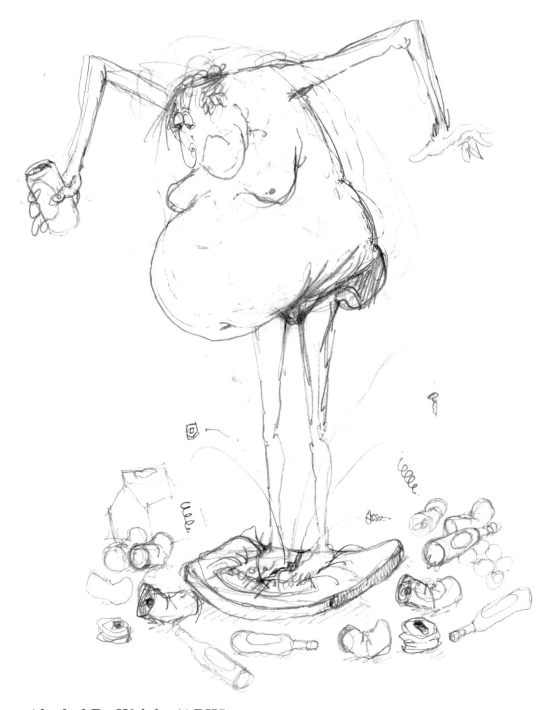

Alcohol By Weight (ABW) \ˈal-kə-hȯl ˈbī ˈwāt\: A measurement used to determine the percentage of alcohol within the beer in terms of weight. Since alcohol is lighter than water, alcohol by weight is lower than alcohol by volume. This measurement is often abbreviated as *ABW*.

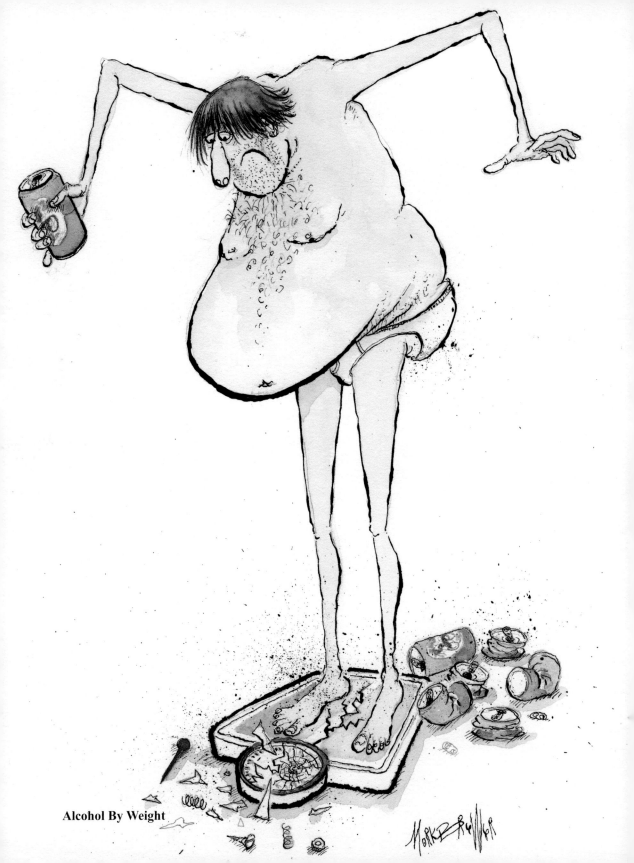

Alcohol By Weight

Ale \\'āl\\: A type of beer produced with yeast strains that ferment on top of the fermenting liquid. These yeast strains typically ferment at warmer temperatures of 59-68°F, although there are yeast strains that ferment at even higher temperatures. This is much warmer than that of the bottom fermenting strains used to produce lagers. Yeasts used in ales tend to produce a byproduct with distinct flavors and aromas of fruits and esters. Ales tend to be served at slightly warmer temperatures than lagers to help enhance these characteristics.

Alpha Acids \ˈal-fə ˈa-səd\: Alpha acids contribute to the bitterness we taste in beer. These acids are found in the flowers of the hops plant. Alpha acids are converted into iso-alpha acids by isomerization when hops are introduced to the boiling mixture of ingredients. These alpha acids can produce a varying degree of bitterness depending on when they are added.

Altbier \ āltbir\: Means "old beer" in German. This style was first brewed in the region of Westphalia. Technically an ale, this style offers a bit of fruitiness with a dark copper to brown color. Commonly it is matured in cooler temperatures, which give altbiers a crisp taste that is more often associated with lagers. As a result, alts are often referred to as "hybrid" beers.

Amber Ale \ˈam-bər ˈāl\: A style produced with a portion of amber malt and other various colored malts to attain a varying degree of copper to light brown color. Many Irish and British pale ales are produced using colored malts to achieve the amber color.

Banana Beer \ bə-ˈna-nə bir\: A type of beer that is light yellow to amber in color and is fermented with bananas. Banana beers tend to have a thinner body with a light frothy head. They are largely produced in Africa but are available all over the world. Banana beer is called *Urwaga* in Kenya and *Lubisi* in Uganda. Typically the aroma of malt and strong presence of bananas is balanced with a taste to match.

Banana Beer

Barley \ˈbär-lē\: A cereal grain used for brewing beer. Once malted, the barley is mashed (often with supplementary grains) in water and heated, which converts the starches into sugars that will be consumed by the yeast to create alcohol.

Barley Wine \ˈbär-lē ˈwīn\: A type of beer with a high alcohol content that rivals that of wine. American-style barley wines are produced with a generous amount of hops to balance this sweetness while creating a bitter taste. European-style barley wines use less hops and therefore are less bitter than their counterparts.

Barrel \ˈba-rəl\: A standard measurement used in the United States that is specifically 31.5 gallons. A barrel may be used to store, ferment, or age the beer until it's ready for consumption. Brewers may store or ferment beer in previously used wine or spirits barrels to extract those tastes, which add to the beer's final character.

Barrel

Beer \ˈbir\: One of the oldest and most consumed alcoholic beverages in the world. Beer is made up of four main ingredients (water, malted grain, hops, and yeast). Together these ingredients are combined with other non-essential ingredients for color, smell, body, and taste, which ferment together before being consumed.

Belgian Blonde \ˈbel-jən ˈbländ\: A variation of a pale ale-style beer often brewed with Pilsner malts that give them a slight sweetness. Belgian blondes are typically yellow to amber in color. They are usually well carbonated and offer aromas of fruity esters with little to no hop bitterness. It is common for Belgian blondes to have a lighter body and a lower alcohol content, although a few of the most popular Belgian blondes have higher ABVs.

Belgian Blonde

Belgian Dubbel \ˈbel-jən ˈdə-bəl\: A traditional monastic-style beer first brewed in the abbeys of Westmalle, Belgium, in the mid-1800s. The name *dubbel* or *double* may refer to the brew being twice as strong as the other beers being produced in the abbeys at that time. Belgian dubbels are typically darker in color and have a fairly heavy body. Traditionally they are low hopped, giving them only a slight bitterness, and tend to have an alcohol content between 6% and 8% ABV.

Belgian Dubbel

Bitterness \ˈbi-tər nes\: The sharp taste in beer often associated with a brew containing an abundant amount of hops. How bitter a beer may taste depends on how long the hops were in the boil (*see* Boil on page 40). This bitter flavor is due to the iso-alpha acids which have been extracted by the process of isomerization from the gland within the flower of the hops plant. The bitterness is measured in International Bitterness Units (IBU).

Bitterness

Black and Tan \ˈblak ən(d) tan\: A type of beer poured in two layers using a light pale ale or lager with a stout or porter. This is possible due to the fact that the darker stout or porter has a lower relative density than that of the ale or lager. A physically layered black and tan is made by first pouring an ale or lager into a glass. Then the stout or porter is slowly poured into the glass over an upside-down tablespoon to avoid splashing and mixing. The earlier and original version of the black and tan still exists and is sold in stores today. It is simply the mixture of a light ale or lager with a stout or porter without being visibly layered. The origins date back to at least the 1800s in England from simply mixing what beer was left over to drink.

Black and Tan

Bock.

Black Malt \\'blak 'mȯlt\\: A barley malt that has been heated in the kiln to the point of carbonization. Black malt can be used in small amounts to deepen the color of the beer or larger quantities can be used in the brewing process to enhance a desired taste.

Bock \\'bäk\\: A type of lager beer that originated in Einbeck, Germany, in the 14th century. It is thought that the mispronunciation of the word "Einbeck," pronounced as "ein bock" with a Bavarian accent is what ultimately led to this beer being called what we call it today. Bock means "goat" in German, so many brewers will incorporate a goat on their label. Bock is a full-bodied beer that is light to dark brown in color and often sweet. Typically it has an above average alcohol content with a malty aroma. Many bocks are brewed seasonally to celebrate various holidays around the world.

Bock

Body \'bä-dē\: The fullness or thinness of a beer's consistency in the mouth. This can be described as a beer having either a thin, medium, or full-bodied taste.

Boil \'bȯi(-ə)l\: A part of the brewing process in which the main ingredients are heated together for a specific amount of time. Boiling allows sterilization to occur, which will remove any unwanted bacteria from the boiling mixture of ingredients. During this boil isomerization will occur, which releases hop flavors that produce bitterness. The boil will extract additional aromas and flavors from the other various ingredients being used as well. Adding different ingredients at different times will produce a variation of flavors.

Body

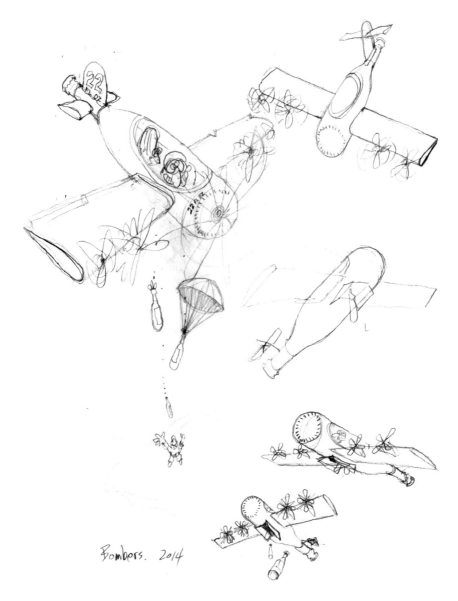

Bombers. 2014

Bomber \ˈbä-mər\: A 22 fl. oz. beer bottle is often referred to as a bomber. Many craft breweries use this size, although less often than the typical 12 fl. oz. bottles.

Bottle Conditioning \ˈbä-təl kən'-ˈdi -shən ēn\: An additional fermentation process in which the beer is allowed to naturally carbonate inside the bottle due to residual yeasts converting sugars into alcohol. Additional aromas and flavors are created during this process as well, which change the complexity and character of the beer.

Bomber

Bright Beer
2014

Bottom Cropping \ˈbä-təmˈkräp ēn\: One of three main types of yeast used in
brewing and the one used specifically to produce lagers. They are also called
bottom fermenting yeasts or lager yeasts. These yeast cells sink to the bottom of
the fermentation vessel where they begin the process of converting the sugars into
alcohol. This happens in much colder temperatures than top fermenting yeast, which
is used to make ales. Bottom cropping yeasts work at approximately 41°F–50°F.

Brewology \ˈbrü-ˈä-lə-jē\: The study of beer, coffee, or tea.

Brewpub \ˈbrü-ˈpəb\: A public restaurant and brewery that sells 25 percent or more
of its own beer on the premises. In 2014 there were over 1,200 brewpubs in the
United States alone with new ones popping up at an exponential rate.

Bright Beer \ˈbrīt bir\: An unpasteurized beer that has been cleared of its yeasts
and transferred into another container. Older, more established breweries
commonly use the term to describe filtered and pasteurized beer.

Bright Beer

Brown Ale \\'braủn 'āl\: A style of beer with a light to medium amber or brown color. The color is indicative of the type of malt used when brewing it. Many brown ales are sweeter, with both a malty and nutty taste, and often are lower in alcohol by volume (ABV).

Bung \\'bəŋ\\: A wooden, cork, or plastic stopper that seals the hole of a cask, keg, or barrel. Beer is poured both in and out of this hole so a tight seal is important.

Bung Hole \\'bəŋ 'hōl\\: The hole in the side of a cask, keg, or barrel that beer is poured both in and out of.

Caramel Malt \ˈka-rə-mel ˈmȯlt\: A cereal grain that has been germinated and then dried in a kiln through a process known as malting. The temperature at which the grains are dried will largely determine the intensity of the malt's color and caramel flavor. Typically caramel malt has a sweet flavor due to the higher concentration of sugars. Malt contributes to the head retention of beer as well.

Carbonation \ kär-bə-nət ˈshən\: The physical fizz, effervescence, or bubbles in a beer. Carbonation can be achieved naturally (bottle or cask conditioning) or by injecting carbon dioxide, or sometimes nitrogen, into the beer at the time of packaging. If sugars are added prior to sealing a brew and left for maturation, the leftover yeasts will naturally convert those sugars into both alcohol and carbon dioxide.

Carboy \ˈkär-ˌbȯi\: A glass or plastic container used by home brewers for fermenting beer. Typically it comes in 3-, 5-, and 6-gallon sizes with 5-gallon being the most popular.

Cask Ale \\ˈkask ˈāl\\: A type of unfiltered beer which is transferred into casks for maturation. Clarifying agents are often used to clear up the beer's appearance before being consumed. Cask ale is naturally carbonated in the cask vessel through the process of secondary fermentation. Once opened, the beer in a cask should be consumed within a few days. It is largely frowned upon when the life of an unfinished cask is prolonged by injecting small amounts of CO_2 into the beer.

Cask Conditioning \\ˈkask kən-ˈdi-shən ēn\\: The process of a beer being transferred into a cask and left to mature until the point of consumption. Prior to consumption the beer goes through a second fermentation process within the cask, in which leftover yeasts convert any remaining sugars into additional alcohol and natural carbonation.

Chill Haze \\ˈchil ˈhāz\\: A cloudy appearance is caused when proteins combine into particles large enough to be seen when reflected by the light. The chilled temperatures cause this reaction, yet it has no effect on the taste of the beer. The haze can be removed by using clarifying agents or finings that will coagulate these proteins so they can be filtered out.

Chocolate Malt \ˈchä-k(ə-)lət ˈmȯlt\: A type of malt used when brewing darker beers to add a roasted, chocolaty, vanilla, or coffee character. Chocolate malt is an essential ingredient to stouts and porters but has also been used for brewing brown ales, dark lagers, and other moderately dark beers.

Clarifying Agent \ˈkler-ə-ˌfī ēn ˈā-jənt\: Also known as finings, clarifying agents are used to clear up the appearance of a hazy beer by coagulating the finer microscopic particles that cannot be removed by filtration alone. Both chemical and natural products, in both liquid and solid form, are used as clarifying agents. The process of adding these clarifiers is called fining. Some natural examples of clarifying agents used in the fining process are isinglass (made from the swim bladders of fish), Irish Moss (made from seaweed), and gelatin. Chemical ingredients used as clarifying agents are aluminum chlorohydrate, calcium hydroxide, iron sulfate, and sodium silicate.

Clarifying Agent

Cloudy \ˈklau̇-dē\: When a beer is non-transparent, due to the intentionally unfiltered yeast and wheat particles or proteins. Most wheat beers are cloudy where lagers appear bright and clear because of the clarifiers that were used to remove particles and proteins that would otherwise cause cloudiness.

Cloudy

Cold Filtered \ˈkōld ˈfil-tərd\: A filtering process in which the beer is chilled to near-freezing temperatures. Doing this enables the leftover proteins to clump together in the beer so they may be easily filtered out.

Cold Filtered

Color \ˈkə-lər\: The hue or shade a beer obtains from the malted grains and other ingredients used in the brewing recipe. Color has nothing to do with alcohol content, and only a little can be realized about the taste based on its color. Lagers and pilsners have a yellow hue and are among the lightest color of all beers. IPAs and saisons are typically a deeper golden yellow while dark lagers and amber ales can look light brown or almost red in color. Stouts and porters have the deepest brown hue and are among the darkest of all beers although the Imperial Stout can almost pass as black in color.

Color

Conditioning 2014

Conditioning \ kən -ˈdi -shən ēn\: The process of leaving a beer to mature following fermentation. There are many ways this process is carried out including leaving the beer in its original fermentation vessel, transferring it into a specific vessel for aging before packaging, and maturing it inside its bottle or keg prior to consumption. Maturing beer in various types of vessels such as steel, wood, and copper all have an effect on the overall taste as well. Temperature also plays an important role in the conditioning process. Conditioning can take weeks, months, or even years depending on the desired outcome.

Conditioning

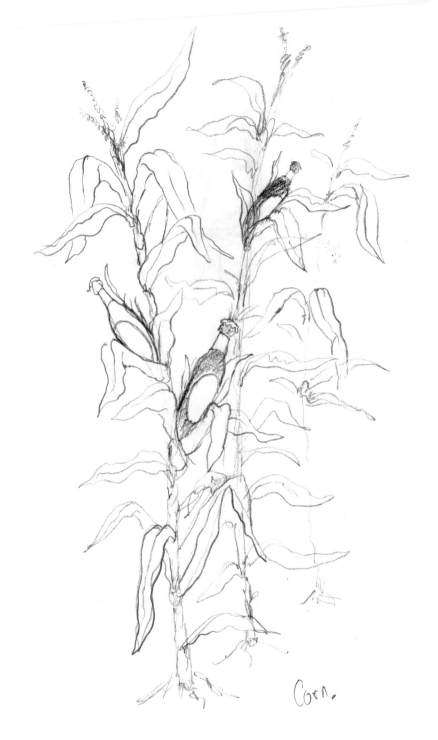

Corn

Corn \ˈkȯrn\: A cereal grain and secondary source of starch for beer. Corn
(maize) is typically used as an adjunct and has proven to be a lower cost
substitute for malted barley. It's commonly used in American light lagers and
pilsners.

Corn

Craft Beer \\'kraft 'bir\\: A term used to describe beer made in breweries that produce beer in quantities of less than 6,000,000 US barrels per year, that are independently owned and operated, and that primarily brew beer. Microbreweries, brewpubs, and regional breweries are all defined as craft breweries. Since the deregulation of small batches of beer brewed at home in 1979, home brewing became popular. This paved the way for many of these beer-brewing hobbyists to open their own craft breweries. Today there is said to be more than 2,500 craft breweries producing craft beer in the United States alone.

Cream Ale \\'krēm ' āl\\: A style similar to an American-style lager, but brewed with ale yeast—although Canadians contributed to refining the taste during Prohibition when American breweries stopped production. Maize and rice are sometimes used as adjuncts to lighten the body. Cream ales are typically light in color and taste with subdued characteristics. Yeasts are used at warmer temperatures for primary fermentation of this ale although it is sometimes conditioned like a lager in cold temperatures.

Crystal Malt \\'kris-təl 'mȯlt\\: A malt that offers a distinct sweet toffee flavor. They are kilned at various temperatures to achieve both an assortment of colors and a varying degree of caramel overtones. Some of the sugars in the crystal malt caramelize during the kilning process which drastically increases the sweetness of the beer.

Craft Beer

Dominant Yeast \ dom-i-nənt ˈyēst\: A strong strain of single-celled
fungi that vigorously influences the taste and character of the beer.
These microorganisms are known as brewer's yeast. Yeasts used for ales
(*Saccharomyces cerevisiae*) ferment on top in warmer temperatures while
yeasts used for lagers (*Saccharomyces uvarum*) ferment on the bottom
in colder temperatures. Lambics are fermented with wild airborne yeasts
(Brettanomyces) while other sour beers use cultivated strains of the same
type of yeast.

Dominant Yeast

Doppelbock \\ ˈdäpəlbäk\\: A type of beer strong in flavor and high in alcohol. The alcohol in a doppelbock typically ranges from 7%–10% ABV or even stronger. *Doppel* or double bock is a stronger beer than that of traditional bocks first brewed in Munich, Germany, by the Paulaner Friars. Because this beer was so sweet and high in alcohol it served as a "meal in a glass" for the friars during their times of fasting. Typically doppelbocks are malty in character with little to no noticeable notes of hops. They tend to be dark yellow to darker brown in color with slight red highlights.

Draft \\ˈdräft\\: Also spelled "draught." Draft beers are dispensed from a sealed pressurized keg injected with carbon dioxide and are typically filtered to avoid sediment. Draft beer from a keg should not be confused with breweries that claim to offer a similar product from a bottle or can.

Draft

Dry Hopping \\ˈdrī ˈhäp ēn\\: The process of adding aroma hops after the boiling mixture of ingredients has cooled and during fermentation. Adding aroma hops during these processes will result in a significant hop aroma rather than contributing to the bitterness. This is because the aroma hops have more beta acids than bittering hops.

Dry Hopping

Dubbel \ˈdə-bəl\: A dark Belgian ale brewed in the monastic style, also called a "double." They typically have aromas of fruit in addition to a malty chocolate-like sweetness. Dubbels commonly have a heavier body and an alcohol content between 6%-8% (ABV).

Dunkel (də ng kl): Any various type of dark German lager. The word *dunkel* itself means *dark* in German. They have a sweet malty characteristic with little or no flavor or aroma of hops. Dunkels range in color from amber to dark brown and have a medium to full body.

Esters \ˈes-tərs\: The organic compounds that yeasts give off, which produces pronounced smells of flowers and fruit in beer.

Ethyl Alcohol \ˈe-thəl ˈal-kə-ˌhȯl\: The colorless yet intoxicating substance found in whiskey, wine, and beer.

Export \ ek-ˈspȯrt\: Any beer that is shipped out of the country. One of the first shipped beers was produced in England for delivery to India. An abundant amount of hops was added to the brew as a natural preservative so the beer would not spoil while in transit. Out of this export grew what we now call an IPA (India Pale Ale).

Extract Beer \ ik-ˈstrakt ˈbir\: A beer made with malt extract ingredients as opposed to brewing with grains and other solids. The fermentable malt extract sugars are in syrup and powder form, making them easier for brewers to use than whole ingredients. Extract brewing is more expensive than all-grain brewing. Many home brewers will choose to produce beer using extracts because less time, expertise, and equipment are needed.

Faro \ˈferō\: A beer traditionally brewed by combining a lambic and another freshly brewed lighter beer called meerts beer. Combining the less expensive meerts beer with a lambic made this beverage more affordable to consume on an everyday basis. Brown sugar was often added for sweetness just prior to serving. Today faro is brewed with lambic and brown sugar and is finished fermenting before it is bottled. By today's standards faro is not considered inexpensive and it is no longer made with meerts beer.

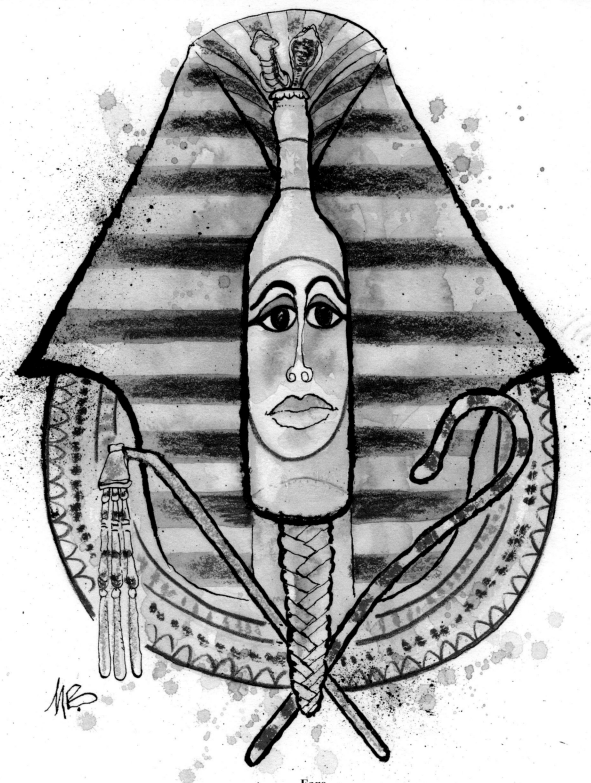

Faro

Fermentation \ ˈfər-mən-ˈtā-shən\: The process in which yeasts convert fermentable sugars into alcohol and carbon dioxide.

Filtered \ˈfil-tərd\: A term used to describe a beer that has been cleared of its yeasts, leftover proteins, and other sediment. A beer may be filtered more than once depending on the desired outcome the brewer wishes to achieve.

Final Gravity (FG) \ˈfī-nəl ˈgra-və-tē\: A measurement of the beer's density (compared to that of water) taken after the fermentation process is complete. Only after measuring the difference in gravity before fermentation starts (original gravity) and then after fermentation ends (final gravity) can the correct percentage of alcohol be calculated.

Final Gravity

Fining \ˈfīn ēn\: Any number of chemical or natural clarifiers that are used to clear up a cloudy beer. Finings (also called clarifying agents) coagulate the microscopic proteins and particles that cannot be removed by normal filtration. The process of adding these clarifiers to clear a beer is called fining. Clarifiers that can be used as natural finings are chitosan, guar gum, and alginates. Chemical clarifiers used as finings are aluminum sulfate, calcium oxide, polyacrylamide, and sodium aluminate.

Flemish Red \ˈfle-mish ˈred\: A Belgian-style ale brewed with a malt that contributes to its red color. These beers are typically sour and acidic with fruit flavors of plum, raison, and raspberry to name a few. They are matured longer than most beers and many times in oak barrels. There is no hop bitterness and they are only mildly carbonated. Many consumers refer to Flemish reds as winelike beers.

Flemish Red

Flute \ˈflüt\: A short-stemmed beer drinking glass with an opening slightly smaller in diameter than the midsection. The tall, slender glass helps maintain carbonation while the smaller opening allows the nose to capture the escaping aromas of the beer.

Flute

Foamy Head \\ˈfō-mē ˈhed\\: The head is the frothy top part of a poured beer. Both hops and malts contribute to the head of a beer and the length of time it will last (head retention). Some draft, or draught, beers are poured with nitrogen and carbon dioxide together. The nitrogen produces finer bubbles which will result in a denser, creamier tasting head than if it were just poured with CO_2 alone.

Forced Carbonation \\ˈfȯr-səd kär-bə-nət ˈshən\\: The act of injecting CO_2 gas directly into beer, rather than allowing natural carbonation to occur.

Framboise \\ ˈfrän-ˈbwäz\\: A type of lambic beer produced with raspberries. Framboise is the French word for raspberry. It is served in a smaller glass than a draft beer. Typically framboise beers are sweet, although other variations are being produced since it has gained popularity in recent years outside of Belgium.

Foamy Head

Fruit Beer. 2014

Fruit Beer \ˈfrüt ˈbir\: A beer brewed with fruits. Often these beers are brewed with extracts rather than using real fruit. Typically the smell and taste of malt and hops are subdued to accentuate the characteristics of the fruit flavor and aroma.

Fruit Lambic \ˈfrüt ˈlambik\: A Belgian-style beer traditionally brewed with real fruit as opposed to syrups. Belgian-style fruit lambics have grown increasingly popular in modern times and are abundantly available throughout the world today. Unlike ales and lagers, which are produced by specific, cultivated yeast strains, lambics are unique in that they are fermented by being exposed to wild yeasts that are native to the area. These yeasts initiate the process of spontaneous fermentation.

Fruity \ˈfrü-tē\: The sweet smell of various types of fruit in beer. The fruity smells may be produced from a specific fruit that was used in the brewing process; however, other ingredients such as yeast and hops produce fruity smells as well.

Fruity

Gluten-Free Beer \ˈglü-tən ˈfrē ˈbir\: A lager or ale made without glycoproteins (gluten), which are found in barley and wheat, the two main grains used in brewing most beer. Often a sweet sorghum syrup that is manufactured from the sorghum grain is used as a replacement.

Goblet \ˈgäb-lət\: A glass that resembles a fishbowl that is typically used for beer with a high alcohol content including German bocks and Belgian ales.

Goblet

Grain Bill \ˈgrān ˈbil\: The types and quantities of grain ingredients used to form the basis of a beer. The grain bill may consist of any number of grains including malted barley, wheat, oats, rice, rye, and sorghum, among others.

Grainy \ˈgrān\: A term used to describe the taste or smell of the grain(s) used in producing the beer. Most beer is made with malted barley although other grains such as wheat, rye, and rice can be contributing factors to a grainy taste and/or smell as well.

Gravity \ˈgra-və-tē\: A measurement of the density of beer compared to that of water taken before, during, and after the fermentation process. Taking readings of gravity throughout fermentation will provide information concerning when fermentation has ended in addition to the percentage of alcohol.

Gravity

Grist \ˈgrist\: Grains that have been milled in preparation for brewing.

Grist Mill \ˈgrist ˈmil\: The building that grinds the grains or the mechanism or machine used to grind the grain.

Growler \ˈgraủ-lər\: A glass or ceramic container (jug) used for transporting craft beer. These containers are commonly sold at breweries to consumers who wish to purchase a craft beer on tap for the purpose of taking it home. The containers are reusable with either screw caps or hinged caps for keeping the beer fresh and carbonated. Growlers come in different sizes although the most popular size is a 64 fl. oz. bottle (US). With the growing popularity of craft beer, consumers can now purchase usable yet collectible growlers from their favorite brewery.

Growler

Gruit \ˈgrü ət\: A combination of ingredients used for flavoring and bittering ale prior to the sixteenth century. This old-fashioned mixture of herbs was applied before the widespread use of hops. Some of the ingredients included in a gruit mixture were sweet gale, ground ivy, horehound, juniper berries, ginger, nutmeg, and cinnamon. Gruit ales were eventually phased out, but in recent years a handful of craft breweries have introduced modern versions.

Gueuze \ˈgoōz\: A Belgian-style lambic produced by combining younger lambics. The fermentable sugars in the lambics allow a second fermentation to occur. Gueuze have citrus, acidic, and musty aromas with a very sour, acidic, and musty taste to match.

Harvest Ale \ˈhär-vəstˈāl\: A style of beer routinely brewed using freshly harvested wet (undried) hops. Using undried hops can produce a grasslike flavor, which is largely due to the moisture still in the hops. Harvest ales may also include ingredients such as pumpkin and nutmeg to reflect the seasonal time of year when they are most widely consumed.

Harvest Ale

Head Retention \\ˈhed ri-ˈten(t)-shən\\: The amount of time the foam on the top part of the beer maintains its stability after it has been poured. A stable head with good retention should last the entire length of time the beer is being consumed.

Head Retention

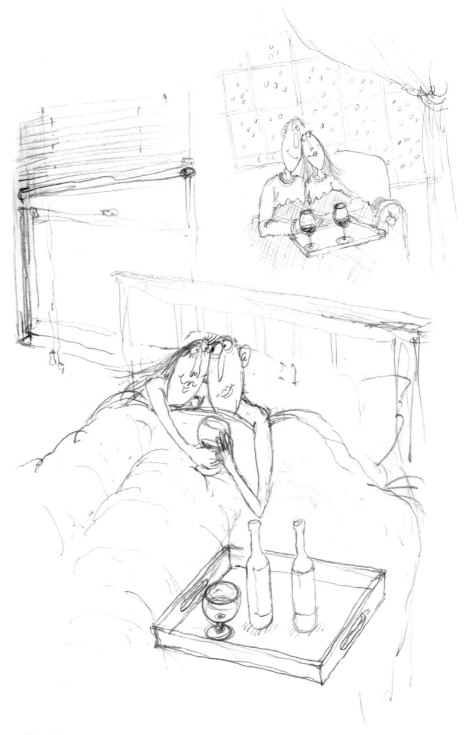

Heat Exchanger \ˈhēt iks-ˈchānj- r\: A piece of equipment or device used to transfer heat from one source to another. Heat exchangers are primarily used to cool the beer to a more suitable temperature before pitching the yeast.

Heat Exchanger

Hefeweizen \' hefə wīz en\: A traditional German-style wheat beer that is well-carbonated, and cloudy in appearance due to unfiltered yeast. The word *hefe* in German means *yeast* and *weizen* means *wheat*.

Helles Bock \'heləs bäk\: A light pale to amber-colored German-style lager traditionally consumed during the spring months. *Helles* means *light* in German. The name was given to distinguish them from dunkels, which are darker in color. Helles bocks are also referred to as heller bocks and maibocks. Besides helles bocks being lighter in color typically they are less malty than dunkels and are brewed with more hops. They still maintain the strength of a traditional bock being no less than 6% alcohol by volume (ABV) in strength.

Helles Bock

Hogshead \ˈhôgz ˈˈhed\: A cask that holds 63 gallons (238 liters) of beer.

Hogshead

Home Brewing \ˈhōm ˈbrü ēn\: The production of beer on a small scale for personal consumption. In 1979, President Jimmy Carter lifted the ban on restricting citizens from creating their own beer at home. Many home brewing starter kits are available for purchase at home brew supply stores.

Home Brewing

Honey Beers.

Aug 2014

Honey Beer \ˈhə-nē ˈbir\: The name given to beer brewed with honey for
its highly fermentable sugars. Using honey is one way in which to keep the
body of the beer light while producing a higher alcohol content.

Honey Beer

Hopback

Hopback \ˈhäp bak\: A container full of hops which the boiling mixture of ingredients is passed through before it is cooled and ready for fermentation. A hopback will not only help retain the maximum amount of the hops' precious compounds that flavor and bitter the beer before fermentation, but will also serve as a filter.

~ Hopback

Hophead.

Hophead \\ˈhäpˈhed\\: Beer consumers who love the taste of heavily hopped
beer. The term has also been widely used for names of beers, organizations,
supply stores, and other establishments.

Hophead

Hoppy \ häpē\: A term used to describe a beer with a bitter taste or aroma. The bitter taste is from hops that are added for bitter flavoring, aroma, and preserving.

Hoppy

Hops \ˈhäps\: The female flower of the hop plant and one of the four main ingredients used in beer. There are various types of hop plants which all have their own unique oils and acids used in the production of beer. Alpha acids are extracted from the hops by isomerization. This occurs when the hops are added to a heated solution, which contributes heavily to the beer's flavor and bitterness. The beta acids in hops do not isomerize; however, they contribute greatly to the aroma. Some hops have more alpha acids in them while others have more beta acids. Therefore, the various kinds of hops have been broken down into two types: bittering hops and flavor or aroma hops. Each are used independently as well as together depending on the desired taste and aroma the brewer wishes to achieve.

Hydrometer \ hī-ˈdrä-mə-tər\: An instrument used to measure the density or gravity of liquid. The alcohol content in the beer can be discovered by taking measurements at the beginning of the brewing process and at the end of fermentation. *See also* Final Gravity, Gravity, Original Gravity, Specific Gravity.

Hops

Imperial Russian Stout \ im-ˈpir-ē-əl ˈrə-shən ˈstau̇t\: A very dark, almost
black in color, full-bodied ale with intense flavors of bitter unsweetened
chocolate, coffee, raisins, plums, and toffee. In addition, Imperial Russian
Stouts have intense, nutty, burntlike aromas and an alcohol content that
typically exceeds 9% by volume. In the eighteenth century they were
produced by Thrale's Brewery in London, England, for export to Catherine II
of Russia. Imperial Russian Stouts are also called Russian Imperial Stouts.

Imperial Russian Stout

India Pale Ale (abbreviated **IPA**) \ˈin-dē-ə ˈpāl ˈāl\: A type of ale with a noticeable although variable bitter flavor. IPAs were widely introduced when an abundant amount of hops were used as a means to preserve the beverage for export from England to India in the eighteenth century.

International Bitterness Units (abbreviated **IBU**) \ in-tər-ˈnash-nəl ˈbi-tər nes ˈyü-nəts\: A scale used to measure the bitterness in beer. The bitterness is due to the addition of hops in the brewing process. Since hops are one of the four main ingredients used in beer almost every beer will have an IBU rating. Beers without much bitterness such as an American lager might receive a lower IBU rating of five (5) to ten (10) while IPAs that have been abundantly hopped might receive a rating of seventy-five (75) or higher.

Irish Moss \ ī-rish ˈˈmȯs\: A form of dried seaweed used as a clarifying agent to clear up a beer that otherwise would have a cloudy appearance. This works by adding the clarifier at the end of the brewing process to collect microscopic particles, proteins, and other leftover solids from the brewing process. Irish moss is often used even when no filtration is done.

Irish Red Ale \ˈī-rish ˈred ˈāl\: A style of beer that is copper to reddish brown in color. Typically they have a slightly sweet caramel malt flavor with aromas of caramel and toffee. The roasted barley contributes to the reddish color and there is little to no evidence of hops.

Isinglass \ˈī-rish ˈred ˈāl\: This is a natural clarifier obtained from the dried swim bladders of fish. Isinglass is used as a fining or clarifying agent to clear particles and proteins that make beer hazy. Isinglass can be used even by those not filtering their beer.

Isomerization \ˈī-ˈsä-mə-ˌrīz ā shən\: A reaction in which alpha acids are extracted from the glands of hop cones. Isomerization occurs once hops are heated in the hot liquid mixture of ingredients. The heat extracts the alpha acids, making them iso-alpha acids. These acids contribute to the bitterness in beer.

Java Stout \ˈja-və ˈstaů̇t\: A type of ale brewed with dark malts that not only give the beer its dark color but produce an aroma and flavor of roasted coffee. Additionally, brewers may add real coffee to intensify the flavor even more. Java stouts are typically bitter and dry in taste. The alcohol by volume (ABV) can range widely from 4% to above 8%.

Jeroboam \ˌjer-ə-ˈbō-əm\: A 3-liter glass bottle. Traditionally wine is bottled and sold in jeroboams, although in more recent years finer beers have been offered for sale in these large bottles.

Java Stout

Keg \ˈkāg\: A large stainless steel or aluminum vessel that contains beer for storing, transporting, and serving. They come in a variety of sizes including ½ barrel (15.5 gal), ¼ barrel (7.75 gal), and ⅙ barrel (5.23 gal). More recently a few breweries are producing mini kegs (5 liters) for retail sales.

Kicked Keg \ˈkikd ˈkāg\: An empty beer container (keg).

Kilning \ˈkiln ng ēn\: The process of drying germinated grains. Drying the grains at different temperatures for different lengths of time will result in various tastes and colors.

Kölsch \ˈkōlsh\: A German-style ale that is top fermented and then aged (lagered) at near freezing temperatures. They are among the lightest yellow in color and have a clear appearance with a crisp, slightly fruity, and refreshing taste.

Kräusening \ˈkrô sen ēn\: A method of conditioning in which refermentation takes place by adding actively fermenting beer that has already finished fermenting. Doing this after bottling will create slightly more alcohol and additional carbonation inside the sealed container.

Kriek Lambic \ˈkrēk lambik\: A style of Belgian beer in which sour cherries or unsweetened cherry juices are fermented with lambics of different ages. The natural sugars from the cherries cause a second fermentation to occur. This produces a dry and fruity, yet unsweetened, sour-tasting beer.

Krug \ˈkrug\: A large and heavy 1-liter German-style beer glass or ceramic mug with a handle. The size and heaviness were first used as symbols to heighten the appreciation of beer.

Lager \ˈlä-gər\: A type of beer fermented in cooler temperatures using bottom fermenting yeast. Lagers are the most commercially available and consumed beer in the world. Much of this is due to the large commercial brewing establishments that have relied heavily on advertising for years to promote their product. The word lager means *to store* in German. Lagers are stored at near-freezing temperatures that help produce a clean and crisp-tasting beer. They are served chilled and vary in color and taste. Common examples of lager beers are pale lagers, pilsners, and bocks, with doppelbocks typically being the highest in alcohol content. Dunkel is a typical dark German lager.

Lager Yeast \ˈlä-gər ˈyēst\: Strains of the yeast *Saccharomyces pastorianus,* named after Louis Pasteur, which are used for making a lager-style beer. These strains of yeast ferment at colder temperatures and are also referred to as bottom-fermenting or bottom-cropping yeasts.

Lagering \ˈlä-gər ēn\: The act of conditioning beer in cold temperatures. During medieval times caves were used to store beer because of their consistently stable cold temperatures.

Lambic \ˈlambik\: A type of dry-tasting sour beer specifically brewed in Belgium and the purest of its kind. Unlike ales and lagers, which are produced by specific strains of brewers yeasts that ferment on the top and bottom, traditional lambics are unique in that they are fermented by being exposed to wild yeasts. These yeasts are native to the area that initiates the process of spontaneous fermentation. Lambics produced outside of Belgium are not true lambics. Many lambics today are consumed after a second fermentation occurs when two younger lambics with fermentable sugars are blended together. Examples of these Belgian-style lambics are gueuze, faro, and fruit.

Lautering \ˈ lôtər ēn\: A filtering process in which the boiled mixture of ingredients is separated from the insoluble grains.

Light Beer \ˈlīt ˈbir\: A type of lager beer reduced in calories and with an alcohol content ranging from 2.8%-4.2% (ABV). They are a very light yellow color, clear in appearance, and highly carbonated, with a well attenuated body and a crisp taste.

Light Beer

Longneck Bottle \ˈlȯŋ-nek ˈbä-təl\: An industry standard American beer bottle with a long neck. They all share the same capacity of 12 US fl. oz., height, and weight.

Longneck Bottle

Lots of Body \ˈläts əv bädē\: A term used to describe a dense beer with a heavy taste.

Lots of Body

Maibock \ˈmī bäk\: A light pale to amber-colored German-style lager traditionally consumed during the spring months. *Mai* literally means *May* in German, although in English is pronounced *my*. Maibocks are also referred to as heller bocks and helles bocks. Besides Maibocks being lighter in color than dunkels, they are typically less malty and brewed with more hops. They still maintain the strength of a traditional bock by being no less than 6% alcohol by volume (ABV).

Maize \ˈmāz\: Another word for corn. Maize is a non-essential ingredient used as an adjunct to the main source of starch when producing beer. Although maize may be used to cut product costs, it is also used for additional flavoring and for creating a foamier head with a longer retention.

Malt \ˈmȯlt\: A cereal grain that has been steeped, allowed to germinate, and then dried in a kiln. Drying the grain for different amount of time and at different temperatures will result in different colored malts. Malt will contribute to the beer's aroma, body, and taste. Malted grain is one of the four main ingredients used in making beer.

Maltose \ˈmȯl-ˌtōs\: A fermentable sugar in malt that is produced by the breakdown of starches. This sugar greatly contributes to the beer's flavor while the yeast will convert these sugars into alcohol.

Maris Otter \ˈmarisˈä-tər\: A specific variety of English two-row barley. This variety of barley was bred by Dr. G. D. H. Bell in 1966 for the sole purpose of creating a high-quality malt to be used for cask-conditioned ales. Maris Otter has superior malting qualities that have made it known as the highest-quality base malt in the world today.

Mash \ˈmash\: A heated mixture of cereal grains and water in which the starches from the grains have been converted into fermentable sugars that make sweet wort, or not-yet-fermented beer.

Mash Tun \ˈmash ˈtən\: A designated vessel where milled grain and supplemental grains (adjuncts) are soaked in heated water. This process is called *mashing*. The mash tun mechanically blends the grains with its mixing rake. This helps to keep the temperature evenly heated so scorching will not occur. Home brewers might use coolers as their mash tun in order to maintain an even heated temperature as they mix the grains by hand.

Microbrewery \ mī-krō-ˈbrü-ə-rē\: A brewery that produces less than 15,000 barrels of beer per year with 75% or more of it sold off-site. As of 2014 there are over 1,400 microbreweries in the United States alone.

Milk Stout \ˈmilk ˈstau̇t\: A type of beer brewed with lactose. The name *milk stout* is attributed to the lactose sugar, which is derived from milk and does not ferment. This attributes to many milk stouts having a sweeter creamy-like taste. Milk stouts are very dark (almost black) in color with flavors and aromas of chocolate and coffee from the use of various malts such as chocolate malt and black malt. Carbonation is low to moderate, and there is little to no taste or smell of hops. Milk stouts have a light brown creamy head.

Milk Stout

Musty \ˈməs-tē\: A term used to describe the smell or taste of a beer. Some lambic beers have a musty smell and taste due to the wild yeasts that are used to ferment the beer. In addition, a musty smell or taste can also be attributed to a bacterial infection.

Musty

Natural Carbonation \ˈna-chə-rəl kär-bə-nət ˈshən\: The fizzy and bubbly results after yeast and sugar ferment in a sealed container. These are called bottle-conditioned beers or cask beers, depending on the sealed container.

Natural Carbonation

Needle Beer.

Near Beer \ˈnir ˈbir\: Any type of beer that was mass produced during Prohibition in the United States that contained little or no alcohol. They were marketed as *cereal beverages* since labeling and marketing it as beer would have been illegal. Near beer is still produced today for those who wish to consume a non-alcoholic beer.

Needle Beer \ˈnē-dəl ˈbir\: Any type of non-alcoholic beer produced during Prohibition in the United States to which alcohol was illegally added. It became common practice to use a needle to inject alcohol through the cork of a non-alcoholic beer bottle or keg.

Needle Beer

Noble Hops \ˈnō-bəl häps\: Four varieties of European hops—Halletau, Tettnanger, Spalt, and Saaz—which offer a low bitterness due to their low alpha acids levels but offer bountiful amounts of aroma. Brewers use this variety of aroma hops for their distinguished characteristics in producing European-style lager beers such as dunkels and pilsners.

Noble Hops

Oast House \\'ōst 'haủs\\: A two- or three-story building built to spread out hops in order for them to dry using a wood or charcoal fire on the first floor. Traditionally many oast houses were converted from cottages or barns. Today more efficient oast houses have been built while the older ones have been converted into homes.

Oatmeal Stout \\'ōt͵-mēl 'staủt\\: A dark ale brewed with a percentage of oats. A bitter or more astringent taste will develop depending on the amount of oats used in the brewing process. Oatmeal stouts have a chocolate or coffeelike character due to the malts they are brewed with. Oatmeal stouts can be slightly sweet yet smooth tasting and have a light brown creamy head.

Oatmeal Stout

Oktoberfest \ äk-ˈtō-bər fest\: The largest fair in the world held annually in Munich, Germany, since 1810. Often called *Wiesn* for short, after where it takes place, this 16-day festival runs from late September to early October, and millions of people from all around the world attend. Only beer conforming strictly to the Reinheitsgebot law is served at Oktoberfest and must be brewed within the local area of Munich, Germany. Only these beers are designated as official Oktoberfest beers.

Old Ale \ˈōld ˈāl\: A traditional English-style ale that is often aged for a long time. Traditionally the name is associated with dark, malty, higher-alcohol English beers that were once sold at a higher price than lesser-aged beers.

Ordinary Bitter \ˈȯr-də-ˌner-ē ˈbi-tər\: A typical English-style ale that is traditionally poured under no pressure using either gravity or a hand pump to extract the beer from the keg. They are golden yellow to copper in color and are lower in carbonation so the head retention is severely reduced. Ordinary bitters have been dubbed *session ales* because they are low in alcohol (between 3%–4%).

Original Gravity (OG) \ ə-ˈrij-ə-nəl ˈgra-və-tē\: A measurement of the beer's density (compared to that of water) taken before the fermentation process starts. Only after measuring the difference in gravity prior to fermentation starts (original gravity) and then after fermentation ends (final gravity) can the correct percentage of alcohol be calculated.

Oxidized \ˈäk-sə-ˌdīzd\: An undesirable stale taste due to the chemical reaction that occurs when an excess of oxygen binds itself with the compounds in beer. This results in an unwelcome rotten or wet cardboard taste. Small amounts of oxidation are appreciated in beers that are aged for long periods of time; however, too much is typically not desirable.

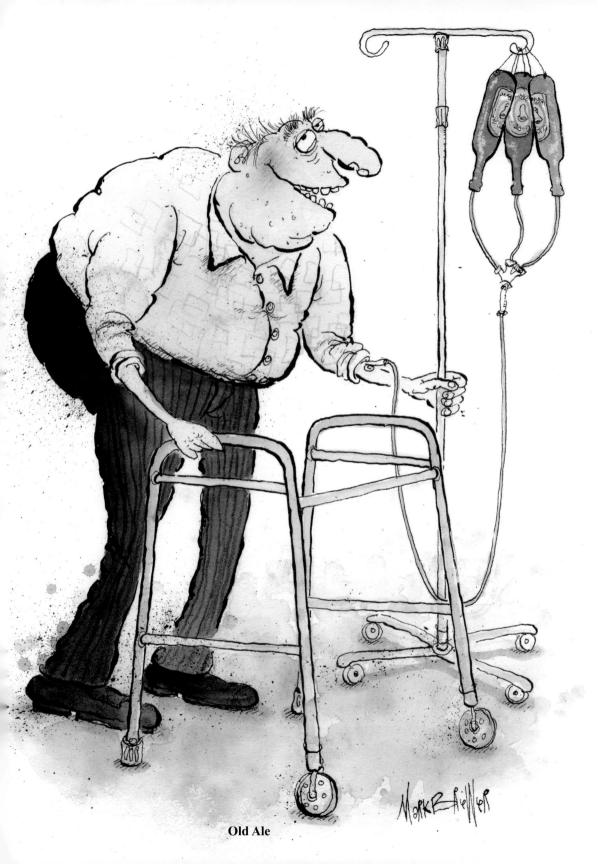

Old Ale

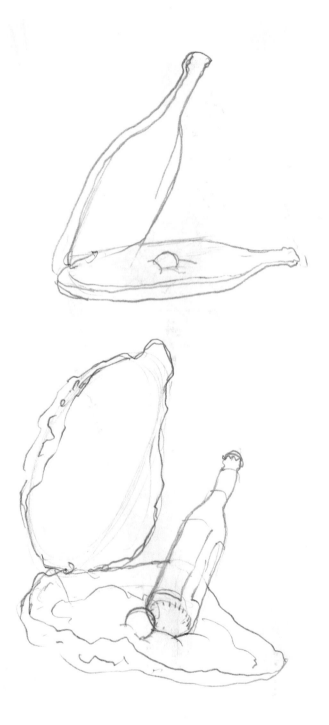

Oyster Stout \ˈȯis-tər ˈstau̇t\: A dark ale either brewed with a handful of oysters but more often just using the name, with the implication that the beer would be suitable for drinking with oysters.

Oyster Stout

Packaging \\'pa-kij ēn\\: The way in which beer is wrapped, protected, and sold to consumers.

Pale Ale \\'pāl 'āl\\: An ale brewed with lightly roasted malts and balanced evenly with the flavor and bitterness of hops. They are golden yellow to copper in color. American pale ales tend to lean slightly more toward the taste of citrusy hops, while English pale ales lean slightly more toward the taste of malt. There are many varieties of pale ales and each with varying strengths of alcohol. Examples of pale ales are blondes, Irish red ales, India pale ales (IPA), bitters, strong ales, and scotch ales, just to name a few.

Pasteurization \\'pas-chə-rə-'zā-shən\\: A process in which a liquid is heated for a specific length of time in order to reduce the number of disease-causing pathogen. Beer may be heated prior to bottling or after to reduce bacteria while many beers are consumed unpasteurized without concern. The process of pasteurization is named after Louis Pasteur, a French microbiologist who worked on perfecting the method in the mid-1800s.

Packaging

Pilsner \ˈpils-nər\: A pale lager beer with an alcohol by volume around 4.5%-5%. Pilsners are both light in color and body and offer a crisp and refreshing taste. They are light to golden yellow in color and have a clear appearance with a distinct hop aroma and flavor. It was first brewed in the Czech Republic in 1842 and the original Pilsner Urquell is still brewed there today.

Pint Glass \ˈpīnt ˈglas\: The most common 16 oz. beer glass with thick sides rising at a slight angle, making the mouth of the glass slightly larger than the base.

Pitching \ˈpich ēn\: The act of adding yeast to a cooled down and well-aerated unfermented beer. Pitching the yeast begins the fermentation process.

Primary Fermentation \ˈprī-ˌmer-ē fər-mən-ˈtā-shən\: The first stage in which yeast starts to convert sugars into alcohol and carbon dioxide. Some beers may be put through a secondary or even tertiary fermentation process before being consumed.

Priming \ˈprīm ēn\: The process in which small amounts of sugar are added to an already-fermented beer. This is done immediately before sealing the beer in a bottle, keg, or cask to induce a secondary fermentation. Once the sugars have been added and the container is sealed the leftover yeast will convert the sugar into alcohol and carbonate the beer.

Prohibition \ prō-ə-ˈbi-shən\: A law once enforced in the United States between the years of 1920 and 1933 that strictly prohibited the production and sale of alcoholic beverages. Dating back to the early 1900s many countries other than the United States experienced their own years of prohibition.

Pitching

Porter \\'pȯr-tər\\: A dark-colored, full-bodied ale that originally had a high alcohol content of 6.6% by volume. Porters have characteristics of chocolate, coffee, caramel, and toffee. The name *porter* was first used in the 1700s and was said to be popular among the hardworking river and street porters of London. The popularity of porters led brewers to produce a wider variety of strengths. This resulted in the creation of single stout porters, double and triple stout porters, and imperial stout porters. Over years the names were simplified to just stout. Modern porters often have a lower ABV, but robust porters and Baltic porters approach or exceed the strength of earlier versions.

Pub \\'pəb\\: An abbreviated term for a public house, which serves beer and other beverages to the public. Also called bars or taverns, pubs are drinking establishments that have been an integral part of many cultures all over the world and for hundreds of years.

Porter

Quaff \ˈkwäf\: To drink quickly or deeply.

Quirky \ˈkwərkē\: Unexpected flavors, aromas, and traits due to the use of unusual ingredients.

Quaff

Racking \ˈrak ēn\: The process of siphoning or transferring a new beer from one storage container to another.

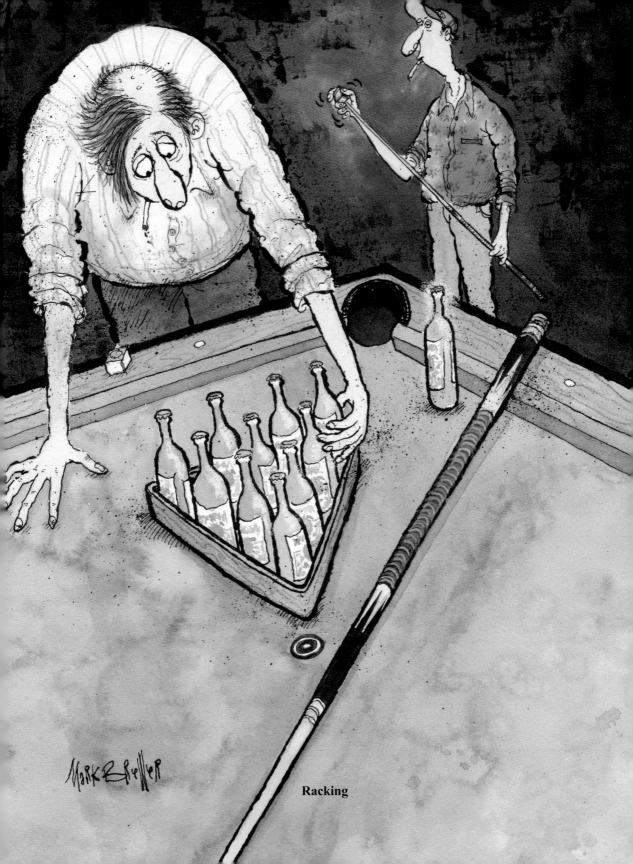

Racking

Radler \ˈra-d lər\: A type of beverage that is made by combining soda or lemonade with beer. The Radler (meaning *cyclist* in German) dates as far back as 1912 and remains a popular drink in many countries including Germany, Bulgaria, Slovakia, Poland, Bosnia, and Romania, among many others. Its thirst-quenching qualities have made it a favorite drink during the summer months. In the United States and the United Kingdom, the term shandy refers to a similar product.

Real Ale \ˈrē(-ə)l ˈāl\: A type of beer that is brewed with traditional ingredients and matured through a secondary fermentation process in the sealed container that it will be consumed from. Real ales are unfiltered and unpasteurized. They are served with only the carbonation that has naturally occurred within the sealed container and must retain active yeasts at the time of consumption. The name was coined in 1973 by a voluntary consumer organization called the Campaign for Real Ale (CAMRA) in St. Albans, England.

Reinheitsgebot \ˈrān hēts gā bät\: A German Purity Law that originated in 1487 by the Duke of Bavaria. The law strictly stated that only water, barley, and hops were to be used as ingredients when brewing beer. This law was put in place for consumer protection. It ensured there would be enough rye and wheat for the production of bread while maintaining the quality and standard cost of beer for consumers. The law has been revised through the years with the obvious addition of yeast to the other three ingredients. Many brewers still comply with the law although today it is largely used as a marketing tool to symbolize purity and a quality standard that still exists in German beers today.

Real Ale

Saison \ˈsī sən\: An ale once brewed in the colder months and with a low alcohol strength that was offered to farm workers in the hot summer months to quench their thirsts. There wasn't always access to clean water so the low alcohol strength was believed to be high enough to ward off disease yet low enough to not slow down the workers on a hot summer day. Today Saisons are still a refreshing summer beer with tastes and aromas of fruit, citrus, and hops but are not always low in alcohol anymore. Saisons ferment at higher temperatures than most beers, between 85°–95°F, and are well carbonated.

Schwarzbier \ˈsh wôrts ˈbir\: A German-style lager beer that is brewed with dark malts to achieve an almost black color. Although they look more like porters or stouts, Schwarzbiers are lagers and lack in yeast flavors with only subtle aromas of coffee and chocolate. Typically the alcohol by volume is between 4% and 5%.

Scotch Ale \ˈskäch ˈāl\: A Scottish type of ale with intense malty aromas and sweet flavors of toffee and caramel. They are light to dark amber in color and have little to no hop bitterness. Scotch ales typically have a full body and can vary in alcohol strength from average to high.

Secondary Fermentation \ˈse-kən-der-ē fər-mən-ˈtā-shən\: Beer that is left to ferment in a sealed container after being removed from the primary fermentation vessel.

Sediment \ˈse-də-mənt\: A byproduct of beer ingredients that settles to the bottom of a keg, cask, or bottle.

Scotch Ale

Session Beer \ˈse-shən ˈbir\: Originally a British term to describe a beer that is low in alcohol. Session beers can be consumed in greater quantities by one person in one period of time (session) without the concern of becoming inebriated. In the United States some have defined session beers to be any beer with an alcohol content between 4% and 5.1% by volume. Others have defined session beers to have no more than 4.5% alcohol by volume.

Shandy \ˈshan-dē\: Any beer (typically wheat) mixed with lemonade and consumed more often during the hot summer months for its refreshing taste. There are different variations of this beverage using slightly different ingredients all around the world. German-speaking countries have been enjoying what they call the *Radler* (*see* Radler on page xx) for centuries. Rather than mixing beer with lemonade they mix beer with a sweet lemon soda water. Shandies are typically lower in alcohol.

Six-Row \ˈsiks ˈrō\: A type of barley that is used in the production of beer. Six-row barley is common in many American style lagers that use adjuncts to supplement the six-row.

Skunky \ˈskən-kē\: Beer with a foul smell or taste due to being overexposed to light. Skunky beers are also referred to as beers that have been *lightstruck* or *skunked*. Cans offer the most protection from light, followed by brown bottles, while green and clear bottles offer little to no protection from the light.

Skunky

Snifter \\ˈsnif-tər\\: A glass used typically for serving brandy or cognac. It is wider at the bottom with a smaller opening at the top and commonly has a short stem. It is used to serve beers like Belgian ales, barley wines, and imperial IPAs to trap in their intense aromas until consumption. In addition, many of these beers are served in snifters because they have a very high alcohol strength, making it irresponsible to serve them in a typical 16 oz. pint glass.

Snifter

Beer in her hand

Specific Gravity (SG) \ spi-ˈsi-fik ˈgra-və-tē\: A measurement of the beer's density (compared to that of water) before fermentation and throughout the process to monitor the decline of gravity. When gravity stops declining, the brewer will know the fermentation process is complete, in addition to knowing the percentage of alcohol content.

Spontaneous Fermentation \ spän-ˈtā-nē-əs fər-mən-ˈtā-shən\: The chemical reaction that occurs when wild airborne yeasts and bacteria inoculate the wort. Belgium lambics have been produced for hundreds of years, specifically using local airborne yeasts for spontaneous fermentation. These wild yeasts are largely responsible for giving lambics a unique and sour taste.

Spontaneous Fermentation

Starch Haze \\ˈstärch ˈhāz\\: The visible presence of unconverted starches in a beer, which gives the beer a cloudy appearance.

Stout \\ˈstaůt\\: A type of ale derived from a porter with an uncommonly dark appearance. The strongest porters were once called stout porters. Since then the two names have been intertwined, which has done little to help clarify the difference between these beers. While porters have intense aromas and flavors of chocolate, toffee, and coffee, stouts have much of the same. Both can be sweet, dry, and have light brown creamy heads. Many stouts have a higher alcohol content than porters, although one of the most consumed dry stouts in the world has a rather low 4.2% alcohol by volume.

Strong Pale Ale \\ˈstròŋ ˈpāl ˈāl\\: A pale ale with a high alcohol content. While many traditional pale ales are lower in alcohol, strong pale ales typically start around 7% alcohol by volume and even go much higher.

Strong Pale Ale

Stubby \ stəbē\: A short glass beer bottle with a little neck. Shorter than most bottles, stubbies are packed and ship tighter than many other bottles. Stubbies first came into popularity in the United States after Prohibition in 1936. Today they have fallen out of style in the United States and have been replaced by the American industry standard longneck bottle, though some modern brewers have adopted them for some of their beers.

Stubby

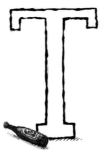

Tap \ˈtap\: A universal word for a faucet or spigot that dispenses beer from a cask or keg by gravity or CO_2 pressure.

Tap

Toasted Malt \ˈtōst ed ˈmȯlt\: A malt that has been lightly roasted to achieve a toasted malt flavor. Kilning or roasting malts at different times and at varying degrees will produce an array of flavors, colors, and other unique characteristics.

Toasted Malt

Top Cropping \ˈtäp ˈkräp ēn\: One of three main types of yeasts used in brewing and the one used specifically to produce ales. They are also called top fermenting yeasts or ale yeasts. These yeast cells float on the top of the fermentation vessel where they begin the process of converting the sugars into alcohol. This happens in much warmer temperatures than bottom fermenting yeasts which are used to make lagers. Top cropping yeasts work most commonly at approximately 59°–68°F.

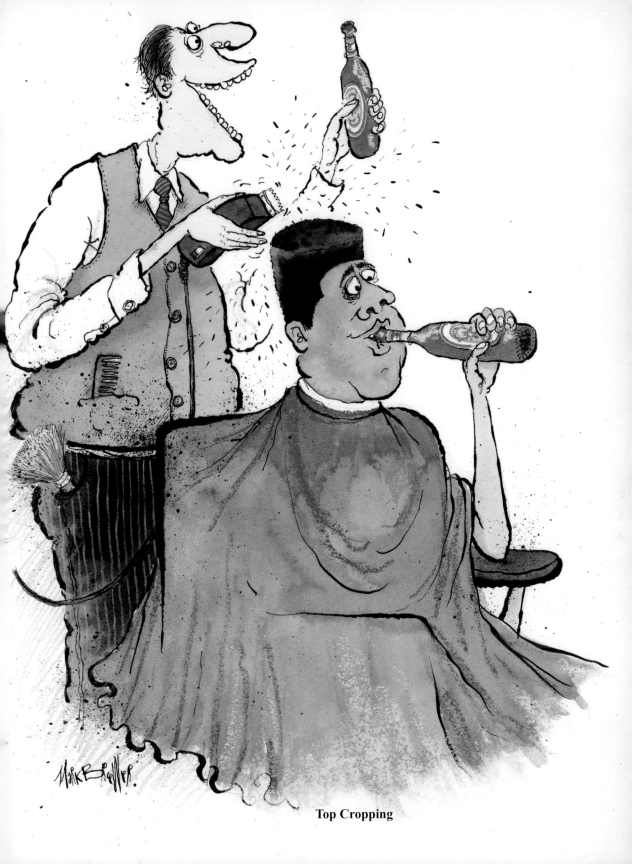

Top Cropping

Trappist Beer \ˈtra-pist ˈbir\: Beer brewed by a brewery in a monastery of the Trappist Order. In 1997 the International Trappist Association was formed. They created an official seal with the words *Authentic Trappist Product* to prevent non-Trappist secular commercial breweries from misusing the Trappist name. Few breweries around the world have been given this highly regarded seal, so consumers can rest assured that if the beer displays *Authentic Trappist Product* it is brewed under the control of the monastic community.

Trappist Style \ˈtra-pist ˈstī(-ə)l\: Any non-Trappist brewery that has marketed their beers as "Trappist-style," without actually being authentic.

Trappist Style

Triple \\'tri-pəl\\: A Belgian ale with a higher alcohol content than that of a dubbel. Made popular by the Trappist Monastery at Westmalle, Belgium, these beers are a deep yellow color and offer an alcohol strength between 7% and 9.5% in volume (ABV).

Trub \\'trəb\\: The layer of sediment at the bottom of a beer fermenting vessel. Trub contains inactive yeasts and proteins that settle after fermentation has ended. To avoid unsettling flavors, the beer is removed (racked) after fermentation is complete leaving the trub behind before it is bottled.

Tulip Glass \\'tü-ləp 'glas\\: A glass with a bulbous midsection and an opening that flares out. The outward flare of the opening helps to retain the head on a beer while allowing the consumer's nose to capture the aromas.

Two-Row \\'tü 'rō\\: A popular type of barley. Traditionally, it was used for English-style beers, yet it is used all around the world today.

Two Stage Fermentation \\'tü 'stāj fər-mən-'tā-shən\\: The process in which a beer is fermented a first time (primary fermentation) to allow most of the alcohol to produce before being removed to finish fermenting in a second vessel. This is done to clarify the beer and minimize or eliminate the chances of the beer retaining any bad tastes from the majority of the sediment in the first vessel.

Tulip Glass

Units of Bitterness \ˈyü-nəts əv ˈbi-tər nes\: A measurement of the hops'
bitterness in beer from the numbers 1–100. International Bitterness Units
(IBUs) are measured through the use of a spectrophotometer and solvent
extraction. The name given to the scale in Europe is European Bitterness
Units (EBUs), which typically measure the bitterness at a slightly lower
value than the IBU system.

Unfiltered \ ən-ˈfil-tərd\: A term given to beers with visible proteins and
sediment purposely left in that are fine for consumption. Filtering a beer
removes a bit of color and some bitterness, while reducing the body which
unfiltered beers typically have. Cask ales are a good example of unfiltered beers.

Unfiltered

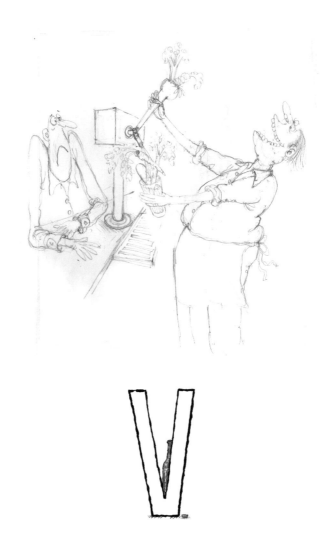

Vegetable Beer \ ˈvej-tə-bəl ˈbir\: A beer that is brewed with vegetables. Often these beers are brewed with extracts rather than using real vegetables. The smell and taste of malt and hops are subdued to accentuate the vegetable flavor and aromas.

Vienna Lager \ vē-ˈe-nə ˈlä-gər\: A lager style of beer that originated in Austria in the 1800s. It is copper to amber in color with a light toasted character due to the roasted malt it's brewed with. Austrian beer makers who immigrated to Mexico in the late nineteenth century popularized the style.

Vinous \ˈvī-nəs\: A term used to describe a beer that resembles the taste and/or smell of wine. Some Flemish ales are described as having smells and tastes that are like wine.

Vegetable Beer

Water \ˈwȯ-tər\: One of the four main ingredients used in producing beer. A beer's taste largely depends on the pH and mineral content of the water that is used. Many breweries pride themselves on the water they use and may even use their water as a marketing tool to sell their product.

Weizen Beer \ˈwizən ˈbir\: A wheat-style German ale with fruity and sometimes spicy tastes due to the various strains of yeast used for fermentation. The word weizen in German means *wheat*.

Wet Hopping \ˈwet ˈhäp ēn\: A term given to a process in which freshly harvested hops are used for brewing beer to enhance the flavor and aroma. Freshly picked hops contain moisture, which is why the word *wet* is used in the term. After harvesting, hops are typically dried out before being used for brewing. Harvest ales use the wet hopping technique to produce a beer that is brewed with freshly harvested hops. In some cases brewers may use these hops only hours after they have been picked.

Wheat Beer \ˈhwēt ˈbir\: A type of ale that is brewed with a large proportion of wheat and is often cloudy in appearance. Typically they are consumed more in the summer because of their refreshing fruit characteristics including cherries, oranges, and lemons.

Whirlpool \ˈhwər(-ə)l-ˌpül\: A term given to the process in which the wort is separated from the solid particles by a means of centrifugal forces that collect the solid and spent ingredients in the bottom center of the vessel.

Whirlpool

Wild Yeast \ˈwī(-ə)ld \ˈyēst\: A name given to natural airborne yeasts. These wild yeasts were used well before any of the more common yeasts that are used now for fermentation. Wild yeasts are used to produce spontaneous fermentation when making lambic beers.

Winter Beer \ˈwin-tər ˈbir\: A name given to beers brewed for consumption during the colder months. Winter beers are also called *winter warmers* and are often marketed as "special" beers for their unique spices or ingredients. Commonly they have a heavier body and are almost always higher in alcohol by volume.

Winter Beer

Witbier \\ˈwit ˈbir\\: A Belgian-style wheat ale that is flavored and also referred to as *white beer* or *wit beer*. When cold, they are hazy in appearance due to the suspended yeasts and proteins that give them a light color some may refer to as white. Rather than using only hops as a preservative, witbiers are often flavored and preserved with orange and coriander, which greatly contribute to the aroma and flavor. Typically these beers are consumed in the summer for their refreshing, thirst-quenching taste.

Wort \\ˈwərt\\: The chosen mixture of ingredients that are boiled together in order to extract various tastes and aromas that will eventually give the brew it's character. This concentrated liquid is typically sweet due to the necessary sugars that are needed for the yeast to convert into alcohol through the process of fermentation. Only after the wort has fermented is it called beer.

Wort

X-tra Hopped \ˈek-strə ˈhäpt\: Beer that has been brewed with an abundant amount of hops to provide an extra bitter taste. A beer may also be marked with the IBUs or EBUs to let consumers know the bitterness.

Yeast \'yēst\: One of the four main ingredients used in beer. Yeast is classified as a fungus with over 1,500 species in its kind. Yeast is used to convert the sugars in the wort into alcohol and then carbon dioxide, thus providing natural carbonation. The three main types of yeast used for brewing beer are *ale yeast*s, which ferment on the top at warmer temperatures of approximately 59°–68 °F (although some ferment at even warmer temperatures); *lager yeast,* which ferments on the bottom and in colder temperatures of approximately 41°–50 °F; and *wild yeast,* sometimes airborne or other wildly occurring yeasts used to produce lambic and other sour beers by spontaneous fermentation.

Zymurgy \\ˈzī͵mərjē\\: The branch of science dealing with brewing and the fermentation process more specifically.